MOTORMANiA

OFF-ROAD VEHICLES

Written by

PENNY WORMS

W
FRANKLIN WATTS
LONDON·SYDNEY

First published in 2010 by
Franklin Watts
338 Euston Road
London NW1 3BH

Franklin Watts Australia
Level 17/207 Kent Street
Sydney NSW 2000

Series editor: Jeremy Smith
Design: Graham Rich
Cover design: Graham Rich
Picture research: Penny Worms

A CIP catalogue record for this book is available
from the British Library.

ISBN: 978 0 7496 9487 6

Dewey classification: 629.2'2042

The author would like to thank Felix Wills and the
following for their kind help and permission to use
images: Jeremy Davey from the Thrust team; Dave
Rowley from the Bloodhound team; and the media
teams at Audi, BMW and McLaren.

Thanks to Felix Wills, Simon Belton at Yamaha Motor
(UK) Ltd, Mark Nevils at Polaris Industries, Urs Eiselin
at Sand-X and Ross Walker at KTM.

Pic Credits
007 MAGAZINE ARCHIVE/EON PRODUCTIONS: 27
bottom (from The Spy Who Loved Me © 1977 Danjaq
LLC and United Artists Corporation. All rights reserved.)
AFP/Getty Images: 16/17 background. James Cheadle /
Alamy: 15 bottom. King Features Syndicate, Inc: 15
centre. KTM-Sportmotorcycle AG: 24/25 all images. Land
Rover: 18/19 background, 18 right. Mitsubishi Motors
Corporation: 20 centre, 20 bottom. National Geographic/
Getty Images: 23 bottom. Polaris Industries, Inc: 10/11 all
images. Sand-X Motors: 12/13 all images. Shutterstock: 6/7
all images, 14, 18 bottom, 20/1 background, 26, 27 centre.
Transtock Inc/Alamy: 23 centre. www.carphoto.co.uk: 17
right, 22. Yamaha Group: 8/9 all images.

Printed in China

Franklin Watts is a division of Hachette Children's Books,
an Hachette UK company.
www.hachette.co.uk

Disclaimer: Some of the 'Stats and Facts' are
approximations. Others are correct at time of writing,
but will probably change.

CONTENTS

OFF-ROAD VEHICLES

Off-road vehicles are powerful and **dexterous**. They can climb and scramble up hills, and can drive through deep ditches or water without damage. Their large wheels or powerful **tracks** can cope with tough **terrain**. They can be fun to drive, too, because whatever nature throws at them, little slows them down.

GAS GUZZLERS

Big off-road vehicles need large, powerful engines that burn a lot of fuel. Many run on diesel because diesel engines are less likely to break down than petrol engines, which is not something you want to do in the middle of nowhere.

4X4

Most off-road vehicles have **four-wheel drive** (known as 4x4), which means the engine drives all four wheels at once. So, if one wheel gets stuck, the other wheels will still turn to get the car out of trouble. Most car engines only drive the front or back wheels.

ACCESS ALL AREAS

There are some places where there are no roads or the roads are not surfaced properly. Rain can turn these tracks into mud. Also, heavy snowfall in some cold places can make roads icy and impassable to normal cars. Off-road vehicles are vital for the people living and working in these places.

ALL-TERRAIN VEHICLE (ATV)

Nippy, light and powerful, the all-terrain vehicle (ATV) or quad bike is used by people who work outdoors and by those who enjoy outdoor activities. They are also ridden for fun and for sport. ATV racing is fast, thrilling and dangerous.

FARMER FUN

The ATV is the farmer's friend. It can power across muddy fields and dusty ground with the speed of a motorbike, but is more comfortable and stable. ATVs are easy to drive and strong enough to pull a trailer. Sheep farmers even use them for rounding up sheep.

SUPER SUSPENSION

shock absorber   *arm*

Most ATVs have an 'independent **suspension**'. This means that the wheels are joined to the body of the vehicle by separate arms. So if one wheel goes over a rock, it doesn't affect the other wheels or cause the vehicle to tip. **Shock absorbers** soak up the bumps, too, to save the rider from a sore bottom!

- **Vehicle:** Yamaha YFZ450R
- **Top speed:** over 120 km/h (75 mph)
- **Country of origin:** Japan
- **Cost:** £8,200
- **Claim to fame:** A motocross winning ATV that you can buy **race-ready**.

RACING QUADS

This 'terrain-swallowing' Yamaha YFZ450R looks like a Transformer but it is actually one of the best racing ATVs. Powerful, lightweight and tough, it is most at home on a **motocross** track, racing other ATVs at high speed.

SNOWMOBILE

Snowmobiles are a vital form of transport in parts of the world where snow is on the ground for a lot of the year. Instead of wheels, they have skis at the front and tracks at the back. The skis steer the snowmobile, while the tracks grip the snow.

SNOW RIDING

The Polaris 600 Rush is a snowmobile built for fun and sport. The Rush is light, agile and powerful. It has a front and rear suspension, so it can speed over uneven snow and land smoothly and safely.

STATS AND FACTS

Vehicle: Polaris 600 Rush
Top speed: over 160 km/h (100 mph)
Cost: from £6,200
Country of origin: United States of America
Claim to fame: It has a unique and advanced rear suspension.

COMFORT TOURING

The Polaris 600 IQ Touring is a snowmobile built for those wanting to travel in comfort. They are heavy and stable, with padded seats and larger fuel tanks. Touring snowmobiles can usually seat one or two people and they have a useful **reverse gear**.

ROLLING TRACK

rear suspension

track

The flat, rubber-like tracks have raised, moulded 'lugs' that act like football boot studs. They dig into the snow to give the snowmobile **traction** or grip. The tracks go round and round, from front to back, pushing the snowmobile forward.

SAND-X

The Sand-X is a tracked all-terrain vehicle that is a quad bike and snowmobile rolled into one. It has two front wheels and a single track at the back. It is mostly a fun vehicle for those living in the desert countries of the Middle East, where sand dunes are plentiful. It is capable of 185 km/h (114 mph) and has such amazing grip that it can do 0–60 in 2.8 seconds!

DUNE BUGGY

The Sand-X is more stable than a normal ATV because it sits very low to the ground and the front wheels are far apart. This means it is not as likely to tip over, and is safe even when powering over steep sand dunes.

STATS AND FACTS

- **Vehicle:** Sand-X
- **Top speed:** 185 km/h (114 mph)
- **Country of origin:** United Arab Emirates
- **Cost:** £16,000
- **Claim to fame:** The Sand-X can do 0–60 faster than a Ferrari Enzo!

ALL-TERRAIN

The Sand-X can travel on **tarmac**, mud and snow, but performs best on sand. It can carry 300 kg (661 lbs) of equipment and its large fuel tank means it can travel over 350 km (217 miles) before needing fuel. That's important when you're in the middle of a desert!

MISSION IMPOSSIBLE

The Sand-X has serious uses, too. It can be used for **border patrols** and search-and-rescue missions in the desert. There is also an armoured version with a gun mounted by the handle bars.

JEEP

Jeep is the oldest name in off-road vehicles. It made its first appearance during World War II (1939–45) as part of the US Army fleet. A war reporter at the time called it 'as faithful as a dog, as strong as a mule, and as agile as a goat'.

WILLY'S-OVERLAND

With the war raging in Europe, the US Army put a challenge out to car makers to produce a 4x4 vehicle fit for war. Willy's-Overland beat Ford with their vehicle, which later became known as the Jeep.

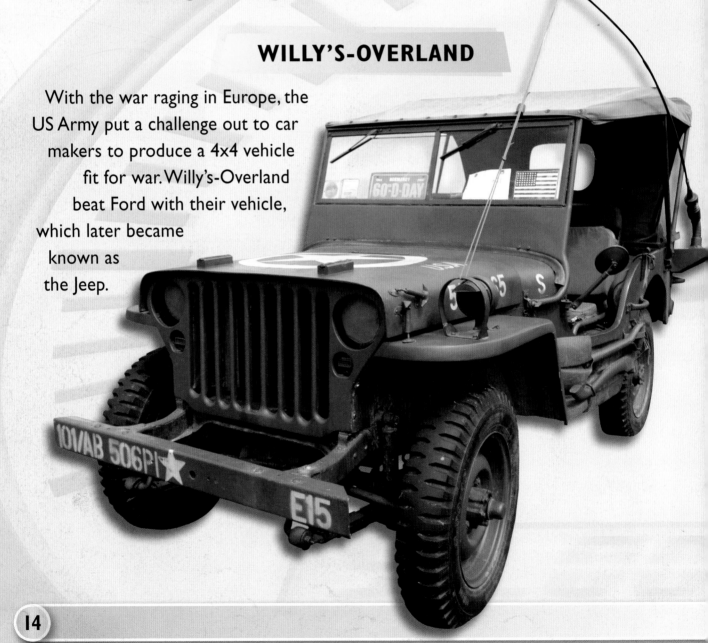

STATS AND FACTS

- **Vehicle:** Jeep Wrangler 2.8 CRD Sport
- **Top speed:** 172 km/h (107 mph)
- **Country of origin:** United States of America
- **Cost:** from £18,600
- **Claim to fame:** A descendant of the oldest and most popular off-road vehicles ever.

EUGENE THE JEEP

The name Jeep seems to have come from Eugene the Jeep, a Popeye cartoon character. Eugene has the ability to appear and disappear, going anywhere he wants to, just like the Jeep. The less interesting story is that the name came from G.P. or General Purpose vehicle.

FUN IN THE SUN

Jeeps have now been replaced by Humvees (see page 16) in the US Army. However, the Jeep Wrangler has become a popular road and off-road vehicle, especially in the United States. They have soft tops and doors that can be taken off for the ultimate open-air driving.

HUMVEE

The High Mobility Multipurpose Wheeled Vehicle, or the Humvee as it is known, is a four-wheeled drive vehicle used by the US Army and other armies around the world. It can drive over deserts, across rocky ground and through jungles safely and for long periods of time without stopping. It is a beast of a vehicle with a great many uses.

CLIMBING AND SWIMMING

A Humvee can climb up a 60 degree slope and can drive at a 40 degree sideways angle. It can go through water up to 1.5 m (4.9 ft) deep. It can tow and haul heavy loads. What it cannot do is go any more than 8.5 km on one litre of fuel (or 20 miles per gallon)!

MULTI-PURPOSE

The Humvee is adapted for many uses – as a troop and equipment carrier, an ambulance, even as a missile launcher. However, the basic vehicles are the same. This is of great benefit to the mechanics who need to keep them in working order.

- **Vehicle:** Humvee M1151A1 w/B1
- **Top speed:** 113 km/h (70 mph) unarmoured
- **Country of origin:** United States of America
- **Cost:** £38,000 unarmoured
- **Claim to fame:** A military vehicle so successful that it is now used by armies all over the world.

THE HUMMER

Hummers are road-going versions of the Humvee. They have the same basic technology. The tyres can **deflate** and **inflate** at the touch of a button when driving. This is useful when driving on mud because flatter tyres have more traction.

UTILITY VEHICLE

Land Rover is one of the most famous names in off-road vehicles and the Defender is the brute of the pack. Comfort is low down on its list of qualities, as is speed. It makes it from 0–60 in an unimpressive 14.7 seconds. But it can climb a hill, wade through water and pull a heavy trailer without breaking into a sweat.

ARMY SURPLUS

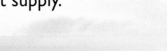

The Defender first appeared in 1948, just after World War II. It was the first non-military utility vehicle but was painted army green because the paint was cheap and plentiful. The body was made from **aluminium** because steel was in short supply.

INDESTRUCTIBLE

Many Defenders went to Africa, Asia and Australia – anywhere where they needed tough cars to cope with bad roads. Over 60 years later, it is said that three out of four Defenders are still running. They are so solid and simply built that it is hard to destroy them. Also, aluminium doesn't rust like steel.

STATS AND FACTS

- **Vehicles:** Land Rover Defender
- **Top speed:** 132 km/h (82 mph)
- **Country of origin:** Great Britain
- **Cost:** from £19,055
- **Claim to fame:** An off-road classic with over 60 years of service.

PICK A STYLE

The new Defender is still a favourite with farmers, explorers, scientists and park rangers – people who need a vehicle that can go anywhere and won't let them down. They can choose different styles depending on whether they need to carry equipment or people or both.

SPORTS UTILITY VEHICLE

The Mitsubishi Pajero is a Sports Utility Vehicle or SUV. It is also known as the Montero or Shogun, depending on the country you live in. Like other SUVs, over time the Pajero has been made more powerful, more refined and more comfortable.

OFF-ROAD

The Pajero has serious off-road **technology**. It has a safety system that controls how the car brakes and the way it grips the ground. There is also a large display telling drivers where they are and at what angle they are driving.

ON-ROAD

The Pajero has been through many changes to make it more city and road friendly. It now appeals to families just as much as the serious off-roader because it is roomy and comfortable inside.

- **Vehicle:** Mitsubishi Pajero 3.2 Diamond
- **Top speed:** 177 km/h (110 mph)
- **Country of origin:** Japan
- **Cost:** from £31,749
- **Claim to fame:** The most successful car ever in the Dakar Rally.

THE DAKAR RALLY

The Pajero is the most successful vehicle ever in the Dakar Rally, a 10,000 km (6,200 miles) endurance race. Originally the race went from Paris in France to Dakar in Northern Africa but in 2008 it moved to South America. The competitors drive all sorts of vehicles, but they must make it across deserts, mountains and extreme terrain.

OFF-ROAD RACERS

There are many off-road races around the world. The Dakar Rally is the most famous, but wherever there is an off-road challenge, there are enthusiasts who will build machines to tackle it. Often, they are made using the best parts from different vehicles.

BOWLER NEMESIS

The Nemesis is as tough as a car can get. Part Land Rover but with all-Bowler suspension and **chassis**, it can tackle all terrain with aggression, agility and speed. If a tyre gets damaged, the Nemesis has a built-in jack to raise all four wheels off the ground so the tyre can be changed easily. And the tyres are about the only thing on this mighty machine that can get damaged!

STATS AND FACTS

- **Vehicle:** Bowler Nemesis
- **Top speed:** 241.4 km/h (150 mph)
- **Country of origin:** UK
- **Cost:** from £120,000
- **Claim to fame:** Bowler are Dakar **veterans**, first with the Bowler WildCat and now with the Nemesis.

WACKY RACERS

In North America, there are many off-road races such as the Best in the Desert series and the Baja 1000. These races attract the real wacky racers – some of the meanest and weirdest looking machines around.

BAJA BUG

The **iconic** Volkswagen Beetle is now a classic car, loved by many. To see one ripping across the desert, sometimes with tyres the size of a truck's, is a mad but common sight in US race, the Baja 1000. They are known as Baja Bugs.

OFF-ROAD MOTORBIKE

Off-road motorbikes are mostly built for racing. Some models are legal on the road, but it's on the dirt where they are really at home. And because they are so light, agile and powerful, they are the kings of any off-road track – going faster than any other vehicle over the steep slopes, hard bumps and tight turns.

KTM 50 SX

KTM are one of the best makers of off-road bikes. They produce bikes for every class of off-road race, all orange and black. The 50 SX is the smallest bike they make. It is used in junior motocross, where competitors can be as young as five years old.

- **Vehicle:** KTM 50 SX
- **Top speed:** not known
- **Country of origin:** Austria
- **Cost:** £2,545
- **Claim to fame:** The 2009 Junior 85cc Motocross World Champion was riding a KTM.

CLIMB AND CONQUER

Motocross is cross-country racing on specially built tracks. The bikes have knobbly tyres that grip the track so they can scramble up slopes. They also have super suspensions for a smoother ride.

ENDURANCE

KTM also build bikes for long-distance enduro races. Enduro is like a car rally, with different stages on a variety of tracks. The engines are quieter and smoother than motocross engines. The bikes are also more comfortable for longer periods in the saddle.

AMPHIBIOUS VEHICLE

An amphibious vehicle is a road-going vehicle that can drive right into a sea or river and magically transform into a boat. The most famous is now 'The Duck'. Ducks are army vehicles that have been transformed into tour boat-buses in some of the world's biggest cities.

TAKE A TOUR

The name of the Duck came from its army name, the DUKW. They were first built by the US Army to carry troops and weapons from ships to land during World War II. Many have been adapted to offer tourist trips around cities, like the one above in Boston, USA. They drive around the city, and then take the tour right into the water.

STATS AND FACTS

- **Vehicle** DUKW (converted)
- **Top speed:** Land/Water 80/10 km/h (50/06 mph)
- **Cost:** £118,000 (to convert from a military vehicle)
- **Country of origin:** United States of America
- **Claim to fame:** DUKWs were used in the **D-Day landings**, transporting 160,000 troops to France!

WHY DOESN'T IT SINK?

The Duck has a watertight **hull**, a **propeller** and a **rudder**, just like a boat. The truck's engine powers a spinning propeller, which creates a force strong enough to move the heavy truck through the water.

UNDERWATER BOND

Probably the most famous amphibious vehicle ever is James Bond's Lotus Esprit in the film *The Spy Who Loved Me* (1977). The Lotus plunged into the water, sprouted fins and a propeller, and transformed into a submarine!

GLOSSARY

aluminium a lightweight metal that resists rust

border patrols when the police and other officials watch over their country's borders to stop people coming in illegally

chassis the metal frame on to which the wheels and body of the car are fixed

deflate to let air out of the tyres

dexterous able to move easily and nimbly

D-Day landings when British, American and Canadian forces crossed the English Channel in boats in June 1944 in order to land on the beaches of Nazi-occupied France

four-wheel drive when the engine of a vehicle powers all four wheels at once, rather than just two as on a normal car

hull the main body of a boat that goes in the water

iconic something that, over time, has become an icon or symbol

inflate to fill up or pump up the tyres with air

motocross cross-country motor-racing on specially built dirt tracks

propeller a circle of blades, like a fan, that is spun round by a motor to propel or push a boat through water

race-ready when a vehicle can be bought and raced immediately, without having to be adapted or strengthened

reverse gear the gear on a vehicle that makes it go backwards

rudder an underwater paddle that is used to steer a boat

shock absorbers air or oil-filled parts that soak up bumps in the road

suspension a system of springs and shock absorbers that work between a vehicle and its wheels to absorb all the bumps in the ground

tarmac a type of material used to surface roads

technology the use of science and the latest equipment

terrain what the ground is like, eg. rocky, smooth, flat or hilly

tracks a revolving metal or rubber band that drives a vehicle such as a snowmobile

traction the way a vehicle's wheels grip the ground so it can drive the vehicle forward

veterans people or vehicles that have seen lengthy and active service

INDEX